mortal fear

mortal fear

meditations
on death and AIDS

john snow

cowley publications
cambridge, massachusetts

Published in the United States of America by Cowley Publications.

International Standard Book No.: 0-936384-49-2

Library of Congress Cataloging-in-Publication Data

Snow, John H., 1924–
   Mortal fear.

   1.   AIDS (Disease)—Religious aspects—Christianity.
2.   Fear of death.   I.   Title.
RC607.A26S62   1987   616.9′792   87-15622
ISBN 0-936384-49-2

Cowley Publications
980 Memorial Drive
Cambridge, MA 02138

CONTENTS

Preface

Things shift and change rapidly in American life. The media pound at our consciousness until we become like computers, numb sorters of input, obediently filing this here, that there, to be retrieved on demand, while helpless to make our own demands on what is to be retrieved. We Americans sit paralyzed by the consequences of our aimlessness. For it turns out that life is not fiction, not a movie. Reality decrees inexorable consequences for the decisions and actions we commit ourselves to. The pigeons come home to roost.

If death is viewed merely as the end of life, a minor chemical event, and life as a kind of survival strategy in a world where all relationships are potentially adversarial, then we are all going to be driven to irrationality or despair. Until we come to grips with our mortality, learning to accept it without denial or despair, until we can fit death into a larger pattern of trustworthy corporate life that provides continuity from one generation to the next, the human enterprise is doomed to the consequences of its own aimlessness.

Two pieces which make up this book were written more or less simultaneously. I was working on the longer piece, *Mortal Concentration* when I was asked to do five meditations at an Episcopal provincial conference on AIDS. The request was providential since it enabled me to stop in the middle of my attempt to work at the agnostic edge of Christianity in order to address the largest possible audience, and to plunge into the heart of my own Christian belief, not as some sort of abstract theological schema, but to address people, largely Christians, who had AIDS, were ministering to people who had AIDS, or were grieving the loss of friends, lovers or family to AIDS.

I cannot adequately express my gratitude to the people who gathered for the conference. Being with them was like waking from a nightmare. No more gamesmanship, no more experts, no more illusion, no more ideology. Just hard truth, exquisite kindness, consistent, shared mutual support, and worship and Eucharist from the heart. We lived together with reality and it was good in Jesus Christ.

As a Black woman priest from the South Bronx who works with young men and women at that terrible vortex where drug addiction and AIDS come together said, "This is the only conference I've ever been to where I am sure, absolutely certain, that I'll see everybody here again."

MORTAL FEAR

AIDS As Disease

We shall gather from time to time during the next three days for meditation and prayers. I've been asked to lead these sessions and I must say that it was something I very much wanted to do. AIDS is one of those things, those rare things met seldom in life, which one must either get to the heart of, dive into the middle of, or ignore completely. You can't flirt with it, fool with it, be clever about it. Either you have to pretend that it is not there, or else that if it is there it has nothing to do with you — or you have to choose to address it seriously, and then only after you have let it speak to your own undefended heart.

I want us to meditate on one different aspect of AIDS at each session. First I want you to meditate with me on AIDS as disease, next on AIDS as a fatal disease, next on AIDS as it defines human nature, and finally on AIDS as it leads us toward a new and vivid apprehension of God.

Americans and disease do not get along very well together. When we wake up with a fever and a sore throat, we are most likely to deny it, to get up and go into the bathroom to prepare to go to work while saying to ourselves, "It's all in my head. I'm fine. There's nothing wrong with me." We take an aspirin. We may gargle. We prepare breakfast and drink our coffee, try to read the newspaper.

1

But the whole time we are sweating. We cannot concentrate on the newspaper, or the television or whatever we use to ease ourselves into the daily round. Finally we say, not really swearing, "Oh Christ! I'm sick."

By this we most likely mean, "There is something wrong with me. I am not fully myself. I have a bug." The disease is our adversary. We have things we must do, perhaps important things. There is of course *work*, first and foremost. Perhaps there are appointments we have to keep, and social commitments as well. We pick up the phone and call in. We are surprised and a little miffed when the boss says, "Stay home. Stay in bed. Don't worry about a thing." We call those with whom we have appointments, or their secretaries, and cancel. We call the people we were to meet socially, our friends. "I'm sick," we say. "Can't make it." "Anything I can do for you? Get for you?" replies our friend. "No," we answer. "I probably just need some rest." "Better see a doctor." "Yeah. I'll call my doctor if I don't feel better by noon."

By noon, the fever has increased and we call our doctor and describe our symptoms. "Well," says the doctor. "If it's anything more than a mild flu, it hasn't declared itself yet. Take aspirin and call me in the morning if you don't feel better. If you get any new symptoms or suddenly feel much worse before then, give me a ring. If you reach my answering service, I'll get back to you before eleven tonight."

And so, having dealt with all our responsibilities in a mature way, we retire to bed and lie there. Sick. If we are married, our spouse is probably at work. We are not only sick, we are alone.

What we have been doing since giving in to our illness is cutting off relationships. We have excommunicated ourselves from the active, industrious, productive well, the truly human group, the group of maximum value. It is alarming how easy this is to do. One minute we are plugged into the interactive process of daily corporate life, not questioning for a moment the security of our place in that life; the next minute we are alone, sick, in bed. The world seems to be proceeding effortlessly without us. We are learning a basic truth, put best, perhaps, by W. H. Auden: "Your being is not necessary." We have ceased to pull our weight, to produce, to maintain, to create. We have become — terrible word — dependent, no use to anyone, and perhaps, eventually, a drag on someone else.

With this realization we may become a bit childish, a bit regressed. "Why didn't the doctor tell me to come right over? Probably could care less whether I live or die, except for his fee, of course. And my spouse, if she cared for me, she would have stayed home. Actually, the whole business of life could go on perfectly well without me. Nobody out there cares whether I live or die, really, unless I'm of some use to them and when I stop being of any use, they can always find someone else."

Doctors have taken to commenting recently on the fact that some degree of depression has for many people increasingly become simply a part of being sick. With high technology, we have nearly programmed mutual care out of our society. What was once expected of us, that we would take the time to care for those close to us who got sick, has suddenly become a nuisance, a burden. It is very hard to stop what we are doing, yet if we have to stop what we are doing to be sick, not many people seem to notice. Could it be that we are committed to such busyness in order to convince ourselves that we are of value to the world?

Within my own memory, there was a time when being sick under normal circumstances confirmed one's value in the eyes of others. We were often surprised to discover how much attention we were given when forced by illness to take to our bed. That was before doctors really understood what was wrong with us, before antibiotics and CAT scans and the rest, when we either got better or didn't get better despite all that medical science could do. In those days, to be sick was to move into an indeterminate state. One was reminded of one's mortality, and so were one's friends and family, and the reality of death bonded all concerned into a caring mutuality. Today, physical illness is simply turned over to the medical establishment to fix quickly — with a pill, a shot, a technical procedure.

Or else physical sickness is seen as a somatic expression — symptom — of psychic sickness. This is particularly true of those symptoms which do not yield to pill or shot or procedure. Sophisticated middle-class people with temperatures and sore throats may ask themselves, "What is it facing me today that I don't want to cope with?" This translation of sickness to the psychic realm has led to another, and I think unfortunate, understanding of sickness whereby it means, simply, badness. If we disapprove of someone's behavior, we may say, "Boy, is he *sick!*" Gay people know all too well how this use of sickness as a moral category masquerading as a medical-scientific category can be applied in the creation of a whole new vicious stereotype.

To be sick today, then, is no simple thing for most of us. We may find it isolating in a number of ways: socially, professionally, psychologically, even morally. Like a car that has ceased to function properly, we are taken off the road and sent to the shop, preferably for repairs. No big deal in most cases. We get better in a hurry. And this is a great blessing. But where this is *not* the case, where the diagnosis is complex and ambiguous or where the diagnosis reveals a fatal illness, the car metaphor continues to hold some truth. The patient, the sufferer, may feel that it is time to be junked, that his or her usefulness is over. In a society as tightly organized and instrumental as ours, simply being sick, *very* sick, quite apart from the nature of the illness, can be close to unbearable. Not only do others, or *some* others, seem to regard us as an excrescence, we ourselves may even come to regard ourselves as being without value.

I have asked you to think about the whole nature of sickness because it is the larger sociological, psychological, economic, and moral context into which AIDS has come. To an alarming degree it is the disease of AIDS which is bringing into sharp focus just how lacking in concern and understanding our society is in this matter of illness. AIDS *does* this. If one does not back away from it, AIDS is like a spotlight into the murky darkness of American life. As we watch our society respond to AIDS, it seems almost to caricature itself. We learn that AIDS may cause a crisis in the insurance industry. We see AIDS researchers holding back new research data in an attempt to beat out their competitors on the world market or for a Nobel prize. Endlessly we hear

AIDS discussed for its economic consequences. We hear that the treatment of AIDS is terribly expensive while AIDS patients linger on unproductive, without income and paying no taxes, making it a national economic problem, and hence, worthy of notice.

All this is to say that AIDS has irrupted into the midst of a system, a human interactive system, without anyone having planned it that way, or planned it at all. We Americans don't plan. What *can* be done will be done. AIDS has appeared in a system which leaves very little room for any illness that doesn't yield to a quick medical fix. Where sickness once made us the focus of attention, it now tends to excommunicate us. Within this system, our value lies in our productivity; it lies far more in what we *do* than in who we are. There are, of course, people who ignore the system and behave towards us as fellow human beings, but these people may put themselves both economically and socially at risk. Those who spend time with the ill remove themselves, often, from a tightly-scheduled social life. When we are sick, we know this, and it does not help our self-regard to have to keep thinking of ourselves as a burden to those who try to be with us in our isolation.

If we stop for even a moment to reflect on all this, we cannot help but be shocked at how far from "Christian" a society that deals with sickness in such a way has become. It happened slowly, inexorably, without reflection or intention. We have come to think of it as simply the way things are, and when we get extremely sick we try to handle it the best we can. The medical treatment part of it (including hospitalization, if we have health insurance) usually works out one way or another, but something may happen to our sense of the general trustworthiness of our corporate life. We wonder if we really have a right to be here beyond our usefulness.

If our disease turns out to be terminal, the sense of excommunication becomes intense. In our empirical, problem-solving society, where it is assumed that if we set the problem correctly we can solve it, we find ourselves in a situation which may have no problem-solving significance. We have no way of thinking about our situation. We are no longer a part of the way in which our society makes sense out of life. Dying, in our society, seems to be something strange, surprising, alien to all we have learned about living. We go on trying to deal with it as a problem, looking for a solution, hoping for a cure, a fix. Or we see the whole thing as somehow a failure, and ourselves as losers — the worst thing we *can* be, as Americans understand life.

It is a shame so many Americans have come to understand life in terms so simple as win-lose. It would be hard to overestimate the pain these procrustean categories have caused us in recent years. They certainly have no warrant from the Bible. Jesus looked at life quite differently. Needless to say, Jesus did not see sickness or death as our society defines them. In a sense Jesus saw sickness as a kind of childlikeness, a state, like childhood, which is a given, where there are no defenses, where dependency is one's due and care is simply an assumption.

Sickness was like a magnet to Jesus. As Jesus — God in human form — was a magnet to the sick. Like children, the sick were without illusion, without defense, trusting him, as

7

the healthy adult with his or her overweening ego so often finds it difficult to do.

Sickness, for Jesus, was simply the human condition made physically manifest, the body declaring its dependency on God to be whole as a physical expression of the soul. Ah. But Jesus *healed* the sick. He healed their bodies. It seems to me that he got tired of healing their bodies. The people whose bodies he healed seldom understood that they themselves had been healed as well, or that they had been healed by anyone but a somewhat more expert shaman. The same self-centeredness which led the sick to Jesus to have their bodies healed they took away with them as healthy persons. Not many even expressed gratitude. Jesus saw that those whose bodies were healed of illness made no distinction between this sign of their salvation and simple biological survival. What Jesus intended them to understand as his power over life and death they took to be their own good luck. Only later was it understood that being cured and being healed were not the same thing. No more the same thing than survival and salvation. It discouraged him how few of those whose symptoms were removed understood what had happened to them, or even who had healed them, who confused their survival with their salvation, their good luck with eternal life.

O God, whose spirit among us is the source of our mutual concern and trust, give us a time to be ourselves without pretension or defense, focus our anger on the structures of our captivity, not on each other; free us from our anxious self-concern and the strategies of our survival to see you in our midst, helping us to love our crooked neighbors with our crooked hearts. Through Jesus our Christ and Saviour. Amen.

AIDS as *Memento Mori*
The Reminder of Our Mortality

Evelyn Waugh somewhere speaks of the languor of late adolescence. Languor, as Waugh understood it, was a healthy and delightful state where one didn't feel like doing much of anything but lying on the grass on a summer afternoon and looking at the blue sky feeling, perhaps, a bittersweet, self-indulgent sadness. One was utterly free of ambition, plans, responsibilities, anxieties, or anything else that might require any expense of energy. One simply *was*. Languor was experienced only for that brief period in late adolescence when it never occurred to one that one would die. Perhaps this kind of languor is best portrayed by Dylan Thomas' character in "Under Milk Wood," Nogood Boyo, who lies on his back in a dory floating in the harbor. He looks up at the sky and says to himself, "I don't know if there's anybody up there, and I don't care."

Languor seems to have disappeared, even during late adolescence. I row a single shell on the Charles River when I get a chance. On a beautiful spring morning I will find young men and women in the boat house rowing as hard as they can row on a machine called an ergometer. On occasion I've asked one of them why they aren't on the river on such a perfect day. "Oh," they reply, panting, covered with sweat, "the Erg is much better. You see, it's scientifically designed to put exactly the same stress on both sides of your body. It equalizes the strength of your left and right arms and legs. If you want to compete you have to row the Erg or you're dead."

"Dead?" I ask.

"Well, you know what I mean. You lose. In competition you have to row a very precise line."

So much for languor. One languorous morning and you're dead.

What a curious use of the word "dead." "If I don't get in the 600's on my S.A.T.'s, I'm dead." "If the Red Sox don't win this one, they're dead meat." Graphic expression, isn't it? To live, to be fully alive, in this view, is to compete. To lose is to die. Even little kids are free with the language of death. And always death is a metaphor for failure. Even a small failure. Death is for losers.

Granted that competitiveness is the criterion for authentic life, life lived fully, there is a deeper assumption here that all relationships are adversary relationships. An assumption like this comes from a simplistic biological theory of natural selection deeply held by most Americans, which we know by the slogan, "the survival of the fittest." The fitness craze, currently affecting a number of young professionals and its commercial exploitation rapidly becoming a growth industry, is not just a fad. There seems to be a surprisingly real commitment and discipline here. So often, when you ask a perfectly fit young person making $75,000 a year, "How are you?" or "How are you doing?" he or she will reply, ruefully, "Surviving" or, "I'm staying alive."

This answer strikes me as somewhat less than enthusiastic. And I suspect that this reply is not merely a question of modesty or self-deprecation, for self-deprecation is not a part of this life-style. Beneath the ironic smile which goes with the reply there is a deadly earnestness. "Surviving" is said with deep pride.

Ronald Reagan, during his first successful campaign for President, was asked by a reporter on television, "Mr. Reagan, many people are asking if it's not irresponsible of you to run for President at your age." The president-to-be smiled and replied, "I don't worry about that. I'm a survivor."

"I'm a survivor." In our society to be a survivor is to be a winner, the best thing one can be. But, I would suggest, it is also to be a loner. To do it, to be a survivor, one makes all relationships instrumental. Even friendship. Even marriage. Any relationship is evaluated by a single criterion: "Does it serve my survival? Is it useful to me? Can I make it work for me and my success?"

A generation born under the threat of nuclear war never knows the delight of languor, has no intimation of immortality, but finds itself trapped in a biological obsession with survival as the most it can expect from life. Life becomes what Hobbes said it would be without reason or hope, the war of all against all. Into this social philosophy, if anything so crudely biological can be called a philosophy, comes AIDS. Suddenly the way most Americans are accustomed to make sense out of life makes no sense at all. It turns out that if biological survival is the end and purpose of human life, and "winning is not the most important thing, winning is the *only* thing," biological survival depends not on planning masterful strategies to get to the top of the heap, not on rigorous exercise and careful diet, but on your immune system. Some idiot virus can blow the whole thing.

Into our competitive system has come something which cannot be set as a problem and then solved. It is an adversary against which we have no defenses and a situation in which there are no winners. This has, of course, always been the case, but with the help of high tech medicine, we have been able to kid ourselves. Surely we would win the war against cancer, with so many millions spent on it. Surely Star Wars, that technological extension of our immune system, would save us from nuclear annihilation. Surely technique could be added to technique until we were finally safe, winners in the war against death. But as it turns out, winning is not the only thing, winning is nothing. It makes no sense out of life at all. Is it any wonder that AIDS has brought such a mixed and confused and at times almost insane response from our society? A society that thought it might have death on the run has discovered or uncovered what we suspected all along and tried so hard to deny. We have discovered that human beings are irretrievably mortal.

Or some of us have. Those with AIDS or ARC certainly have. Those who have been found to carry AIDS antibodies have. Those at risk have or have not; they have either proceeded with a frantic denial or have decided to take their mortality seriously, to look at mortality as a simple given of being alive rather than as some surprising, inexplicable, and unfair intervention by an evil force. Is how good the same as how much? they ask themselves. Is the quality of life the same as length of life? Are all relationships simply useful or useless, to serve my advantage or my pleasure or else to be dissolved? Is everyone potentially my adversary? How important is the customary ordering of our life together, our corporate life? How important is morality—not simply straight middle-class morality, but the inclination of all serious people to find fair and helpful customary ways of dealing with our life together? Does our mortality give an added urgency to our being trustworthy and faithful people, or is it simply a good reason to say, "To hell with it. Go for it!"?

That a single group, largely of gay men, has found itself brought face to face with this *memento mori* in the most forcible way should not leave the straight majority free to trivialize it. AIDS has a way of not letting itself be trivialized. As more and more straight people discover that men on whom they depend, men whom they trust and love as friends and colleagues, have AIDS and are in fact homosexual, their ability to trivialize, deny, and forget about AIDS will decrease. They will see that what is happening calls out to them for seriousness in their own lives.

Jesus brought his disciples to the consciousness of death as an inevitable part of the human condition in a memorable encounter with Peter, reported in the Gospel of Matthew.

Peter has just identified Jesus as the Christ, the Messiah, the Son of the living God. (Mt 16: 21-26)

From that time Jesus began to make it clear to his disciples that he had to go to Jerusalem, and there to suffer much from the elders, chief priests, and doctors of the law, to be put to death and to be raised again on the third day. At this

15

Peter took him by the arm and began to rebuke him. "Heaven forbid!" he said, "No, Lord, this shall never happen to you!" Then Jesus turned and said to Peter, "Away with you, Satan; you are a stumbling block to me. You think as men think, not as God thinks."

Jesus then said to the disciples, "Those who wish to be followers of mine, must leave self behind; they must take up their cross and come with me. Those who care for their own safety are lost, but those who will let themselves be lost for my sake will find their true selves. What does anyone gain by winning the whole world at the cost of the true self? And what can anyone give that will buy that self back?"

Jesus said it clearly. The self which has not accepted its own mortality is not a true self. We Christians are not immortal. But we have been raised from the dead.

There is a difference here that is not simply a piece of theological esoterica. The doctrine of immortality of the soul has always carried with it a temptation to identify the body with the flesh, to see the body as something separate and somehow less than the soul, as a perishable burden with which the soul is afflicted until it is freed by death. Although evidence for the doctrine can be found in the New Testament, it doesn't seem to be at the heart of what either Jesus or St. Paul taught about death.

Both regarded human beings as all of a piece. It is the fear of death which makes us imagine this split. The body in pain and weakness, the body slowly or suddenly turning, so to speak, against itself, losing its magnificent, complex, incomprehensible, energetic grace and balance, its responsiveness to event, its expressive genius, its beauty, its unique configuration of variables that make it not only all of a piece but one of a kind—the terrible, particular loss of this body is not some simple chemical phenomenon. No empirical explanation of the process can trivialize the loss. The process and our consciousness of the process are one. Who we *are* is dying, not some inconsequential part of us. It is our body which is related to the human corporate whole and to the whole of creation, related to history and its redemptive movement through time towards a loving God. Out of the miraculous dust of the universe we come crying into the world to become the unique and particular human bodies we know as ourselves, bodies in no way different from the body God chose to inhabit when God came to share the human lot. In our mortal fear we try to imagine ourselves out of ourselves. We seek objectivity, distance, serene autonomy. But to no avail. To be reconciled to our mortal bodies is to be reconciled to ourselves and to one another and to the creatureliness which God loves and claims and welcomes at the end, through Jesus Christ our Savior.

Grant us, O Lord, to trust in you with all our hearts: for, as you always resist the proud who confide in their own strength, so you never forsake those who make their boast of our Mercy. Through Jesus Christ our Saviour who lives and reigns with you and the Holy Spirit, One God, now and ever. Amen

AIDS As Fatal

For those who don't have it, AIDS is a reminder of their mortality; they can respond to it in a variety of ways or try to ignore it altogether. For those who *have* AIDS some of these options are reduced. They can interpret what has happened to them in different ways, they can tell themselves different stories about their pain, but the fatal nature of AIDS is a simple given. In this respect AIDS is like life. The only totally predictable thing about it is that it will involve suffering and it will end.

Education in America tends to teach us to ignore the unpredictable. What is important is quantifiable, measurable, and, if *not* predictable, would *be* predictable if we knew more, if we understood its rules better.

All of the rules of predictability, of science, have been applied to AIDS. Rigorous research has revealed what causes it, how it affects our immune systems, what the most likely symptoms will be, and some statistical probabilities about how long we can expect to live once we have the disease. When all of these facts are in, if we have the disease, we still have been told nothing of any significance at all. It would be totally different if the disease were curable, for then these facts would be the only significant data. Put them all together and they spell health. Put all the facts about

AIDS together and we have a heap of facts. Nothing more for the person who has AIDS.

Some time ago I had a colonoscopy to remove some polyps from my colon. Before the procedure the doctor and I went through a brief ceremony called informed consent. Before I gave my consent to the procedure I was informed of the risks of the procedure. After receiving the information I was to give my consent by signing a paper which freed the hospital of responsibility for any of the bad outcomes which I had been informed were possible. The doctor told me that the chances of the scope penetrating the wall of the colon were one in three hundred. All I heard was that the scope might penetrate the wall of the colon.

The doctor told me that there was a ten to twelve percent chance that the polyp might be malignant. What I heard was that there was a chance the polyp might be malignant. Even where there was a *possibility* of a fatal disease or a life-threatening mistake in the procedure, empirical, quantified, predictive information was of little help to me. I could say to myself, "Gee, my chances are pretty good," but somehow it didn't help all that much. Numbers are cold comfort.

Now what I did do as the doctor went on and on with his numbers was to scan the walls for his credentials, to see where he had gone to college and medical school, to see what his professional memberships were. I was busy trying to convince myself that I had the best G.I. specialist in America, perhaps in the world. What I did was to regress, to become a child searching for an omnipotent and omniscient parent who could do no wrong and who would take care of me. In recent years doctors have become suspicious of this kind of response from patients. We're told that we should take charge and manage our own illness, make our own therapeutic choices from information the doctor provides. The doctor is not there as a surrogate parent to infantilize us; he is there to provide us with the best information so that we can function as responsible adults.

The doctors are no doubt right about this, but the concept is not terribly helpful. Unfortunately, people cannot feel a certain way on demand. It is not helpful to tell someone not to regress, not to be childish, not to have impossible expectations, mainly because this is what most of us do as we move towards life-threatening situations — major surgery, chemotherapy, and the rest — where in the end we are *not* in charge of our own lives.

What one learns, as a Christian, is that what we have come to regard psychoanalytically as regression, as childishness, can become childlikeness. It can become the acceptance of one's ultimately dependent nature as a given, not as a form of pathology or cowardice. Unless you become as a little child, you will not enter the kingdom of God. Without something like regression, we cannot pray. With all of our defenses up and our energy focused on survival, we may be able to repeat the doctor's information verbatim and we may even be able to make clear therapeutic choices. Yet going on beneath the rational exterior is a lot of fear and anger which will surface if, suddenly, there are *no* more choices, if, as it turns out, the last choice has been made.

If one can accept one's regression, if one is not made to feel ashamed of one's dependency on unrealistic expectations of the doctor, one can then make the next step. Those childish expectations are put where they belong, upon the living God, the one who cares about what happens to us and has the last word in the matter of our mortality. Where this happens we can hear and act on the doctor's information with the most clarity of all. Yet far more important, with this we have moved into a radically new relationship with God in Christ. I do not mean by this the total assurance of one's ultimate safety in God's hands at all times, from day to day, a total absence of fear. What I mean might best be described as slowly learning the virtue of patience, that most un-fashionable virtue of all in our time.

Patience comes from the Latin word, to suffer. A patient is one who suffers. Patience is, according to the Oxford English Dictionary, "the calm abiding of the issue of time, the quality of expecting long without rage or discontent." All that makes patience possible is trust. Calmly abiding the issue of time requires a certain confidence, the confidence of a child in a trustworthy adult. It requires confidence, cer-tainly, in one's doctor, but it is confidence that must go beyond the doctor if we are truly to be healed, to be made wholly ourselves as we accept ourselves as God accepts us, as dependent and mortal and incomplete until we are completed by death and reborn in Jesus Christ, our Saviour.

When Jesus died, his last words according to the Gospel of John, were "It is finished." The Greek word here translated "finished" means a good deal more than something coming to an end. It means "completed," brought to a purposeful end. Perhaps the most difficult thing about dying from AIDS is the overwhelming sense of randomness and waste that most often goes with the death of a young person. How can anyone find here a sense of purposeful completion? Isn't it more like a meaningless accident? Not unless we consider it so.

In the past we have prayed for time to die. We have asked God to deliver us from dying suddenly and unprepared. The extraordinary thing about human life is that where we let God turn our life around, time becomes kind of irrelevant. A life that has drifted, or has even been malevolently focused for thirty years, can take on an extraordinary qualitative purposefulness and a kind of radiant significance in a few months, touched by grace. When our lives are completed in Christ, they are ready for eternal life.

O God, the protector of all who trust in you, without whom nothing is strong, nothing is holy: increase and multiply upon us your mercy: that, with you as our ruler and guide, we may so pass through things temporal that we lose not the things eternal. Through Jesus Christ our Saviour, who lives and reigns with you and the Holy Spirit, One God, forever and ever. Amen.

AIDS And What It Means To Be Human

Now I want to reflect a little on AIDS and on what our response to it reveals about our doctrine of human nature. I have already talked at some length about our tendency to regard the human individual as a competitive biological unit. I think this probably defines most accurately how we feel about ourselves when we are most under stress, particularly in situations where the stress is related to competitive situations which we view as win-lose. Yet there are other stress situations which reveal who we believe we are in more complex terms.

For all of our enjoyment of being sharp and fit and achieving and competitive, there are moments even when we're at the top of our form when we sense that we have lost something, something that has to do with belonging, with community, with membership. One may be a gifted team player and able to work with others to compete or achieve, but there is an occasional let up in one's instrumental interaction when one asks, "Is technique all? Does all my value lie in my skills and my usefulness for some task, often a task for which I feel no special affection?" There is that sense of something lost. A brief memory of family closeness and safety during childhood, perhaps. Perhaps a moment in a church worship service during early adolescence. It is always a memory of self related in a non-competitive way to other selves, often in doing something purposeful which was itself non-competitive. Often we enter into psychotherapy with the intention of recapturing this sense of noncompetitive belonging. We pay the doctor not to one-up us, but to listen to us, to care about what happens to us, to take us seriously simply as who we are, as we work together to make who we are more like the person we would like to become.

For we are social creatures, most ourselves when we are serving and being served by others to some good end, an end we have chosen and which is precious to us.

Gay and lesbian people know a good deal about all this. In the days before the whole matter of homosexuality came out of the closet, when homosexuality was regarded by a straight society as simple immorality and psychiatry had not yet come to present it as a form of pathology, gay and lesbian people were experts on alienation. The guilty secret seemed an insurmountable barrier between them and any felt sense of safe belonging, or trustworthy community. They seemed doomed to excommunication at some deep, mysterious level from the moment that they revealed this secret to themselves. As a result they couldn't take the issue of community and belonging, their social selves, for granted. Many, of course, were simply destroyed, accepting society's definition of who they were as the last word. Others chose to serve the society which rejected them. Some made the choice to do this out of a religious context, others out of a determination to survive, realizing that society would be less likely to destroy them if they were indispensable to it. They learned to do things essential to our common life and to do them exceedingly well.

I remember an older gay friend telling me, "We knew that we wouldn't find any lasting happiness or fulfillment in the realm of sexuality. Society had destroyed that whole area of our lives. We dealt with it the best we could, but our commitment and energy went into our work and our friendships. If we were artists or poets or musicians our commitment and our deepest satisfaction was in our art. If we went into something else, we made a point of understanding the whole context of what we were doing, its structure and politics and interpersonal dynamics. We kept our eyes open, we had to in order to survive, we knew exactly what was going on. People called us gossips, but many an enterprise would have collapsed without the flow of information which we provided."

I myself can vividly remember getting out of the service after World War II to return to college on the G.I. Bill. Shortly before college opened I got a letter from the Veteran's Administration informing me that they had no record of my military service. I tried the telephone first and got shunted from one flat voice to another until finally, after twenty minutes, there was just silence. I hopped on the subway and went to the V.A. office and it was more of the same. I would be referred to someone and I would wait. I could see the person to whom I was referred drinking coffee and joking around with other bureaucrats as I waited to be seen. When I was called to his desk there would be no eye contact, only an arrogant shuffling of papers and weighty silence and then a referral to someone else who knew nothing.

Finally I lost my temper completely and started shouting. The recipient of my rage looked startled, got up from his desk and disappeared. He returned shortly with another man, large, cheerful-looking, a homosexual, who immediately started joking me into a better state of mind. He listened carefully to what I said, looked closely at the documents I had thrown on the desk, made three phone calls, and presto, all was taken care of and I was a bona fide veteran again and eligible for the G.I. Bill. I don't know how many times I have been submerged in a church bureaucracy, an educational bureaucracy, a bank bureaucracy, only to be rescued at the last moment by someone gay, thoughtful, knowledgeable, and *helpful*, paying attention to me as a person, willing to put out, to go to some lengths, to serve my particular needs.

I think these encounters had a lot to do with my reluctance to accept the medical dictum that homosexuality was a form of illness. If these cheerful, competent, helpful, indeed, loving people were sick, who is healthy? In a very real sense the gay bureaucrat, the gay hospital attendant, the gay barber, or for that matter the gay teacher or professor, or priest, are so often islands of animated health in a sea of apathy and demoralization. I suspect this is so because gay and lesbian people don't take belonging and community, the social dimensions of the self, for granted. They know the pain of excommunication and have for the most part little desire to contribute to it.

But there is a dark side to all this, too. People who have based their value, and indeed, their very security and survival on active, animated competent service, have a lot of trouble with being terribly sick. The fear of being abandoned, rejected, treated as no longer useful, is intensified. This fear is not restricted to homosexuals, either, for it is more and more prevalent among straight people as well. AIDS has brought this fear to issue, has brought the breakdown of trustworthy community to issue in a way that must be addressed, particularly by the Christian churches.

It seems to me that where the church fails us, to the extent that it does fail us in our culture, is in trying to make itself useful. The church as community builder, as change agent, as continuity giver, as a source of mental or physical health, is a church obsessed with results, with success, a church desperately trying to prove its usefulness in a society which talks incessantly of the bottom line. The intention of the church in all these endeavors is good and worthy, but something essential is likely to get lost when it perseverates in doing good, often explicitly stated and deeply understood as "problem solving." The church has not proven itself in the past to have been a particularly good problem solver.

The primary and essential purpose of the church is the worship of God, as God is revealed in Jesus Christ. This is why we gather into this very worldly institution. This is what begins our coming together and sustains what unity we have. Our commitment to the church is a commitment to this worship, and to the God we worship.

Where worship is eucharistic, we engage ourselves in acting out a narrative which defines who we are in relation to God and each other and to the world. Our behavior in the Eucharist is voluntary, intentional, reflective, just, sharing, corporate, healthy, globally aware, forgiving and reconciling. And, in a curious way, it is political as well in that we give our consent to the ordering and leadership of our corporate worship. Our behavior in the Eucharist is not merely loving; it defines what loving is.

Worship is the most useless of all human enterprises, and consequently the most free. We do it because we choose to do it, not for any particular pay-off. Its results are unpredictable. It is full of surprises, although in its ritual it is and should be thoroughly predictable. Eucharistic worship permits us to enter a powerful vision of reality, the order behind the accidents where even pain and death become a part of human dignity subsumed in the glory of the eternal God. In the Eucharist our value simply as God's creatures, children, friends, is not questioned, but established and blessed. The Eucharist does not tell us what to do, it does not solve our problems. It simply lets us be, in time and out of time, what we were created to be.

The value of being human is radically questioned today, not on a conceptual level, but on the level of social and institutional practice. If we examine this practice, the closest thing to a cultural consensus would seem to be that humans have value to the extent that they are competitive, that is, fit to survive. If we regard humans simply (oh, too simply) as vulnerable organisms in a dangerous environment, this is not altogether wrong. We must, when it is appropriate, assert ourselves as individuals. A more humane answer, a deeply religious and certainly Christian one, is in being servants, in realizing the social dimension of the self and serving one another in our life together.

But the Gospel of Jesus Christ goes beyond this to the very source and image of our being. W.H. Auden in a poem, "Epistle to a Godson," wrote, "Be glad your being is not necessary." Be *glad*. To us today, this is nearly incomprehensible. "Make a difference!" we are told. "Don't be a part of the problem, be a part of the solution." I've heard that one from the pulpit. "When the going gets tough, the tough get going!" "Be glad your being is not necessary." How difficult it is to believe that we have a right simply to be, to be here and now exactly as we are. The God of the New Testament revealed in Jesus Christ does not demand credentials or a resumé. This God, a poor Jewish carpenter's son, the ruler of the universe, made us for himself. To be whole, to be healthy, to be saved, is to realize, whether we are sick or well, growing or dying, right or wrong, happy or full of anguish, that we belong at some deep, eternal level to the God who made us, who suffered and died to bring us home. This is the most important thing about being human. This is the Good News.

Most loving God, whose will it is for us to give thanks for all things, to fear nothing but the loss of you, and to cast all our care on you who care for us. Preserve us from faithless fears and worldly anxieties, that no clouds of this mortal life may hide from us the light of that love which is immortal, and which you have manifested to us in your Son Jesus Christ our Saviour. Amen.

A New Apprehension of God

I want, finally, to reflect on AIDS as it leads us towards a more vivid apprehension of God.

In recent years the Episcopal Church has been much concerned about its spirituality. Many priests and lay persons have taken to retrieving an old practice called spiritual direction, where two people, one usually with some special training, work together to deepen their prayer lives. To the extent that a method is involved in this practice, more emphasis than is usual in Protestant Christianity has been placed on meditation, a kind of wordless meditation, a meditation without specific content and aimed at becoming entirely free of content, at becoming a kind of self-emptying, leaving us free of "faithless fears and worldly anxieties" to be addressed by the very presence of God.

The interest in this form of prayer was sparked in many people through an interest in Buddhism. These people could see no reason why Buddhists alone should know the peace of this kind of prayer, and discovered that in fact Christians, particularly the monastics, have been engaged in this sort of prayer since the earliest days of the church. What such prayer requires is that we do something with our ego, our self, that precious center of our consciousness and will that we think of as uniquely us. The Buddhists see the goal of the practice as simply doing away with ego, something which doesn't exist anyway, by their view. We Christians are less inclined to get rid of ego, since we believe that it is precious to our creator God. We would rather see the ego drop its posture of self-defense, turn off its security systems, and open the door. Maybe what's out there isn't so scary after all. Maybe it's God.

I've never been much of a one for meditation. I envy people with the concentration and discipline for it, but if I tried to clear all the junk out of my head it would take the rest of my life. It's very busy up there and I've had to learn to sneak through the traffic. I gave up on inner peace and tranquility long ago to become a kind of spiritual artful dodger.

But all this emphasis on spiritual direction and some of the reading I've done about it have been helpful to me in understanding what for me have become spiritual basics.

I have during these meditations often mentioned the extent to which our culture regards the fear of death as the only healthy motivation for a progressive and growing society, how we emphasize constantly that survival, in its various disguises of winning, victory, success, excellence, being number one, is the only trustworthy motivation for the energetic, creative, imaginative building of a free world. We are taught to regard competitive fitness as the key to freedom, and individual freedom as the highest human value.

Yet the author of the Epistle to the Hebrews looked at it rather differently.

"The children of a family share the same flesh and blood: and so he too shared ours, so that through death he might break the power of him who had death at his command, that is, the devil; and might liberate those who through fear of death had all their lifetime been in servitude" (Heb. 2:14-16).

If we can believe this epistle, those whose primary concern is their own survival spend their lives in slavery to the devil. The devil, the king of non-being, the father of lies who controls his subjects by convincing them that death has the last word, is the one who keeps us from God. The New Testament's most powerful metaphor for sin is captivity to the fear of death. Those ruled by the fear of death will do anything to stay alive, will obey anyone or any idea that promises them survival. We tend to see anyone or anything who promises us a stay of execution as a savior. From the point of view of our present value system, a God who died for us seems pretty fragile if we compare this God to Star Wars, which Caspar Weinberger keeps insisting is the only hope we have.

It seems to me that all fear comes in the long run from the fear of death. The ego, the conscious, willing center of our being, will make self-defense its primary concern until it becomes reconciled to its own mortality. The agent of this reconciliation for Christians is the Holy Spirit. This is why we are so afraid of the Holy Spirit. We do not *want* to be reconciled to death. We depend on our fear of death to force us to be survivors and winners. Without it, who would we be? What would motivate us? If we weren't afraid of death, why would we keep fighting to do away with nuclear war? If we weren't afraid of death, what would motivate cancer research, or for that matter, AIDS research? And so it goes. We find it difficult to imagine a society that does not have survival as its primary motivator, and even less can we imagine ourselves reconciled to our mortality.

I don't think we have to worry about losing our fear of death. We won't. What AIDS is teaching us spiritually is what the world knew until the nuclear age, when the knowledge became unbearable and we forgot it, which is that a culture healthy for human beings mitigates the fear of death, constantly, by its customs and rituals. Rituals remind us that death is an integral part of the human condition and only slightly more to be feared than other moments of transition in human life. A life ruled by the fear of death is no life at all. Something new is being opened up here, or else something old that we have allowed to get lost may be in the process of being recovered.

The person who lives by the denial of death lives captive to the fear of death, with no conscious need for God, knowing no reason why God should exist, having no evidence that God does exist. The person captive to the fear of death through denial is spiritually blind. AIDS has brought our mortality out of hiding, and made it very difficult to deny. Unlike nuclear war, it is not a vague threat out there in the maze of high technology. It is among us, killing some of us and some of our friends, leaving us randomly vulnerable to our environment, making us terribly, manifestly mortal. Suddenly the fact of our mortality is undeniable and we are afraid. But in recovering this mortal fear we recover our humanity as well. Our humanity is created by the God who loves us, the humanity which is such a precious gift when we accept it and are reconciled to it in its wholeness, including death. The acceptance of mortality is the beginning of patience, "the calm abiding of the issue of time, the quality of expecting long without rage or discontent." Patience is the climate, the environment of prayer, and it is in this environment that the presence of God may become vivid through the Holy Spirit. Without the fear, trying to deny or avoid the fear, we deny ourselves the consolation as well. Without the cross, there can be no crown. Without the death of the autonomous ego in the disintegration of mortal fear, there will be no resurrection.

"The children of a family share the same flesh and blood: and so he too shared ours, so that through death he might break the power of him who had death at his command, that is, the devil: and might liberate those who through fear of death, had all their lives been in servitude."

And what God freed us for is clear. To love one another as God in Christ loves us.

O God, who by the glorious resurrection of your Son Jesus Christ destroyed death and brought life and immortality to light: Grant that we, who have been raised with him, may abide in his presence and rejoice in the hope of eternal glory; through Jesus Christ our Saviour, to whom with you and the Holy Spirit, be dominion and praise forever and ever. Amen.

MORTAL CONCENTRATION

Depend upon it sir! When a man knows he's to be hanged in a fortnight's time, it concentrates his mind wonderfully.

Samuel Johnson

I. SURGICAL STRIKE

Some events seem to shape one's life more than others. This is an attempt to reflect on such an event. A somewhat delayed physical examination, which should have taken place three years before, followed by a sigmoidoscopy, followed by a lower G.I. X-Ray, revealed a large polyp in my colon. Arrangements were made for a colonoscopy which took place four months later, an excruciating procedure followed by a two-day wait to discover whether the polyp were malignant or benign.

All this covered a period of four intensely busy months during which time I was engaged, as a seminary professor, in teaching, preaching, correcting final papers for my courses and together with my wife moving from a twelve-room faculty house to a three-bedroom condominium and, on the same day, delivering a paper to the Maturity Studies Institute on the midlife crisis and the reconstruction of theology. The colonoscopy took place three days later.

A remark that Samuel Johnson made to James Boswell kept coming into my mind, something to the effect that the knowledge that one was going to be hanged in a fortnight's time tended to concentrate the mind wonderfully. This observation of Johnson's turned out to be very true for me. Yet the world during this period was eventful enough to break even such mortal concentration — not really to break it, perhaps, so much as to diffuse it through my sermons, my paper on midlife and theology, all idle moments of fantasy as well as more intentional periods of contemplation and prayer.

During these four months, as I said, events in the world kept breaking in to my consciousness. I cannot remember the sequence of these events, and somehow the sequence doesn't seem important to me. Indeed reason, in the empirical sense, was not helpful during this period, at least during those rare moments when I resorted to it. Ten to twelve per cent of colonic polyps are malignant. The chances of the scope penetrating the wall of the colon while the colonoscopy is going on is one in three hundred. This information from the "informed consent" procedure, along with the form from the hospital I was required to sign, freeing the hospital from all responsibility for any sort of bad outcome, did not help me put anything in "rational perspective." Perhaps the Russians are right. Don't tell anybody anything if you can help it. It is a rule of Russian medicine that the doctor never tells patients they have cancer. To do otherwise is regarded as cruel. Yet in all fairness to my doctor, most of the information given me was in answer to my own questions. Indeed the doctor expressed surprise at my questions. "No one ever asks me those questions," he said, looking rather worried, I thought. Perhaps he believed I was looking for a malpractice suit.

Looking back on the whole business now I realize that from the first lab report at the beginning of the four months or perhaps even poking around in my excrement to provide data for the lab, my way of looking at life changed. Not radically. Not dramatically. But the way I looked at things was somewhat altered by the intensification, the *slight* intensification, of the awareness that I was mortal. As I looked at the large and surprising events I found reported on television or in the newspaper front page, I began to see a curious and novel equivalence holding them together. Things took on a metaphorical significance they had not had for me before.

During that four month period the first event to shake me up and get my attention was President Reagan's long, inexplicable article in the *New York Times Magazine* about the Mafia. Everything I knew about colonic polyps I had learned from media coverage of Mr. Reagan's own colonoscopy, with its unfortunate outcome. Our parallel experience kept Mr. Reagan on my mind, and I read the article with great interest and some alarm. Clearly the Mafia, or the Mob, or organized crime (Mr. Reagan or his collaborator tried desperately to make the Mafia sound as un-Italian as possible) was of obsessive concern to the president, a cancer gnawing at the very bowels of American society which could bring us down if we did not root out every vestige of it. It was pure evil, and the president was very worried at the passivity of the American people, expressed in their view that the Mafia would be always with us because it exploited such basic human frailties. This notion, the president said, was a cop-out. Without the conviction that the Mafia could be rooted out (surgically removed?), we would not exert the massive effort necessary to save America.

The president also seemed to believe that the Mafia appeared out of nowhere in Chicago in the Twenties, invented, so to speak, by Al Capone. History was not the article's strong point; neither was sociology nor any kind of disciplined thought. Yet clearly the passion was authentic.

I thought back to my own experience with the Mob. During the late Forties I had lived for two years on Mulberry Street, near Prince. I had graduated from college and dutifully come to New York to look for a job, as one was supposed to do in those days. Fortunately my old roommate was just leaving his eighteen-dollar-a-month apartment on Mulberry Street to go to Spain, and turned it over to me. There was a recession at the time and few jobs, so I registered, as a veteran, for the 52-20 club (twenty dollars a week for fifty-two weeks) and settled into the apartment to begin what turned out to be a discouraging and increasingly apathetic job search.

Evenings I didn't spend drinking with friends at the San Remo on MacDougal Street, I spent playing the piano for beers at Cappy's Bar on the corner of Mulberry and Prince. When Cappy's closed I would occasionally be invited to the Italian American Club across the street, where I would listen to my Italian neighbors talk about life in a most unguarded way. I learned a lot, not a little of it about the Mafia, or the Mob, as my neighbors called it. I never heard the words "Mafia" or "Cosa Nostra" used. As far as I could see, the Mob was a kind of ethnic territorial security force which had been brought from Sicily by some very oppressed people and adapted in an organic way to meet the needs of immigrants attempting to defend themselves from exploita-

44

tion in a new locale where they were held, by the powers that were, in contempt, only marginally served by the laws and the economy in which they found themselves. By the late 1940's, most Italians I knew on Mulberry Street were beginning to feel nervous about the Mob. Yet they were not convinced that they could do without it. It provided a kind of security and social equilibrium and a degree of power over their lives where they were which, along with the church, made them feel safe. Yet it also embarrassed them by its violent image. Publicity about the Mob's strong-arm enforcement policies tended to separate them from the larger opportunities of American life — opportunities increasingly open to them as, through the G.I. Bill, they became better educated and more secure away from their own turf.

What surprised me most was how important territoriality was to the Mob. If you lived in the neighborhood and were friendly and kept your nose clean, you did not have to be Italian to benefit from the security the Mob provided. The streets were safe, the kids, adolescents included, were polite and respectful, the food was good and cheap, your car wasn't ticketed, the streets were clean, and if you suddenly got into trouble you knew help was close by. If you made trouble, got mean drunk, were aggressively on the make for neighborhood women, were rude to the elderly or did anything illegal without the Mob's knowledge and permission, you might be warned once, but the second time it would be too late. The Mob, like Mr. Reagan, had a tendency towards overkill. The key to a very happy and secure life on Mulberry Street was prudence, and learning the rules so you could *be* prudent. Basically, the Mob was the expression of a community's search for that most elusive and addictive of all values, security.

The late Gregory Bateson had a theory about addiction. Addictive behavior, according to Bateson, is adaptive behavior which persists long after the circumstances which made the behavior adaptive in the first place have changed. By the 1940's the Mob was beginning to move from being adaptive to being addictive. What the immigrant community had developed to help them survive was no longer really needed for their survival. Loan sharking was soon to be taken over by the banks. The numbers racket was no longer needed as Italians found a more secure place in an upwardly mobile economy. So the original purpose the Mob had been created to serve became murky, but the Mob kept doing its thing (Cosa Nostra) to no social purpose and in the process became more hurtful than helpful to the Italian community and to society at large. Like an alcoholic pouring out larger and larger drinks as he approaches the bottom of the bottle, the Mob has ceased to serve anyone (including itself) as its illegal activities have grown in scope and destructive power until it has become isolated, and alone, and headed for extinction. Indeed, it has become rather like cancer, where cells that were once part of the immune system become the enemy of that for which they once provided security, and on which their own life depends.

Mr. Reagan is a great one for the surgical strike and doing away with evil once and for all. Security is his middle name. One cannot help but wonder whether that curious article on the Mafia was not the work of a man trying in some oblique way to deal with his own cancer, which for one his age is a particularly urgent *memento mori*. One thinks of the grand cliché of the cancer surgeon pulling off his mask and saying, "Of course I can't say for sure, but I think we got it all. If anyone can come through this, it's you. You're a fighter. A real survivor." "Come on America. Give it all the fight you've got and we can get rid of every trace of the Mafia. We can get it all!"

Another attempt at the surgical strike that took place during my four months of mortal concentration was the bombing of Libya. The point of Libya was to rid the world of terrorism and to begin by going after "state-sponsored" terrorism. Colonel Khaddafi, aided by ex-CIA agents and moonlighting American Special Forces trainers, supplied with the most sophisticated American explosives and equipment, had been training terrorists in Libya. If the terrorists had spent their time killing Arabs or bombing an occasional department store in London or coffee house in Paris, this would presumably have been all very well and good, a fertile field for free enterprise exploitation. But the President's attempt the previous year to keep peace in Lebanon by sending in marines utterly untrained in peacekeeping duty and, of all things, a battleship to protect them, changed all this. Americans were no longer perceived as peacekeepers, but as Israeli allies; suddenly Americans became the focus for some hideously effective terrorism.

Intent on ridding the world of terrorism, the president decided that Libya was *the* national base for much of the world's terrorism, and staged two high tech attacks on the Libyan mainland. A whole naval task force with carrier succeeded in sinking a patrol boat and its crew and wiping

47

out a radar station, the most expensive piece of military surgery in history. The second attack was a technical wonder, with planes flying all the way from England over Spain to Tripoli and back with the loss of only two men and one plane, and of course with planes from the carrier doing their bit as well. This, too, was announced as a surgical strike by a government spokesman on TV. Using our superbly sophisticated electronic equipment we had taken out precisely those targets we had planned to take out in advance, including the embassy of one of our European allies, as it turned out the next day, and an alarming number of civilians: women, children, the elderly. Some of Khadaffi's children were wounded. His adopted daughter was killed.

Following this attack, there began one of the more bizarre periods in American history. Hundreds of thousands of Americans canceled their flights to Europe, or whole summer vacations in Europe. American embassies all over the world became armed fortresses. Airports, even American airports, doubled and tripled their security. In order to avoid terrorism, some tourists decided to tour the Soviet Union, one group arriving in Kiev just in time for the explosion at Chernobyl. European heads of state hastened to meet with representatives of President Reagan and agree to anything he wanted them to do about terrorism. Yet by then, European heads of state had learned something about President Reagan. If you publically agree with him on anything, that is all you have to do. He will quickly lose interest in anything once he wins, once he perceives himself as perceived as having got his way. For the president, the winner image is all. He really asks nothing of anyone but the appearance of success. The terrorists, in the mean time, have succeeded beyond their wildest dreams. The bombing of Libya has proved more disruptive and expensive to the Western industrial nations than all the terrorism that took place before it. There is no need for the terrorists to risk a thing for the time being. There is no way they could improve on or amplify the terror in the West, a terror which has no empirical basis whatsoever in terms of the individual's statistical risk.

The only real risk is that President Reagan will decide to root out some new evil with another surgical strike, and this time the Russians, really scared, will show less restraint than they have so far.

The risk, seen from one point of view is the risk of maximizing rather than optimizing a single variable in a large, complicated open system. One cannot deal first with terrorism and ignore the economic, political, diplomatic, cultural and moral context within which terrorism takes place. Indeed, the unpredictability of large open systems, their vulnerability to the impulsive behavior of key human beings became all the more a part of my mortal meditations when the space shuttle Challenger exploded. I watched it on television as voices from the space center described in curiously abstract language what their instruments registered had happened.

I find space launches inexplicably beautiful and moving. Like most Americans, I had ceased to worry about the danger involved in these launches, but in my peculiar spiritual state, a kind of interim state, I had been worrying all morning about the icicles, the cold weather, all the dangers which informed TV commentators had plainly warned of before the launch.

Then I heard of the explosion before a class, and when the class was over rushed to a television to see a replay — which was no replay to me. My stomach churned. I began to sweat. All of my vague anxiety focused into fear and I began briefly to shake. I'm good at suppressing feeling and soon had myself under control again. Except for a kind of irritability, an only partially submerged anger.

Usually I rather pride myself on not kidding myself, on not depending much on denial to defend myself. One cause of my anger was the realization of just how deep my denial went. I suppose what brought the fear I had been denying to the surface with such force, even though I knew what I was going to see, knew already what had happened, was my growing distrust of my immune system. Perhaps there was a polyp. Perhaps it was malignant. Perhaps my own fail-safe mechanism was faulty.

Teilhard de Chardin maintained that the more complex a system, the more conscious it is. Von Bertalanffy, the great German biologist, in his General System Theory holds that large complex systems which can adapt to their environment and adjust and change to deal with unexpected input are also less predictable, are "low-probability" systems. A closed, relatively simple system like a stable atom, is very predictable; it is a "high-probability" system. One can predict with great accuracy what will happen to a stable atom in time. This is not true of the weather, a lowprobability system where the wings of a butterfly in South America could theoretically cause a hurricane in New England, granted the right set of circumstances. Neither is it true of a human being.

In order to maintain their homeostasis, the integrity of their function, all systems are equipped with negative feedback mechanisms, smaller systems within systems which monitor new input and destroy or keep out new things which the system might not be able to assimilate to its own advantage. Examples of negative feedback mechanisms are endless. In nature, most creatures have a negative feedback function within an ecosystem. In other words, hawks monitor rodents, carnivores monitor herbivores, birds keep down the insect population. And so it goes. Perhaps the most complex negative feedback system in nature is the human immune system, which goes far beyond its genetic gifts to become conscious and learned. Humans learn and remember what they can and cannot eat, what hurts and what doesn't, what is dangerous and what isn't. They learn what to risk and what not to risk. Perhaps the basic ingredient of the conscious human immune system is rationalized fear, a very complex form of negative feedback which can itself go awry and move into paranoia and crippling anxiety. Denial and other psychic defenses such as suppression, repression, projection, and the rest serve a negative feedback function to maintain the rational dimension of fear and keep it from breaking into a paranoid runaway. I showed up on time for my colonoscopy by simply suppressing my fear of the danger and the pain I knew would be involved. I didn't think about it. Much.

According to Gregory Bateson, the Industrial Revolution really began when Watt applied the principle of negative feedback to the steam engine. Watt had no way to regulate the heat under the boiler with any precision. If he threw water on the fire the engine stopped. If he didn't, the engine went faster and faster until it exploded or flew apart. It then occurred to him to regulate the steam pressure rather than the fire by a simple negative feedback device, the governor, which was set to release steam from the boiler as necessary to maintain a steady speed. The same principle is most familiar to us today in the thermostat, which sits on the walls of our dwellings and keeps them at a steady temperature.

It is interesting that from the beginning human beings have experienced technology as an extension of themselves. I can remember as a child standing by a steam locomotive for the first time when it suddenly seemed to explode. I began to cry. "Don't worry," my father reassured me, "it's just letting off steam." Later, when my father seemed to explode, my mother would say, "Don't worry. He's just letting off steam." Psychiatrists call it ventilating.

The principle of negative feedback, of building monitoring and controling mechanisms into systems, made it possible to increase not only their scale and efficiency, but with the addition of electricity, also their complexity and sophistication. The purpose of increased complexity was, presumably, to serve the human endeavor by extending human capabilities. Basically, technology was to be the extension of our corporate immune system, a kind of sacramental rationalization of nature that would reduce its unpredictability, make it more manageable, and thus less demanding and dangerous to the human enterprise. Like the Mafia and the early Italian immigrants, it was an adaptive expression of our need for security in an environment perceived as hostile and dangerous, exploitative of both our time and energy.

Yet technology, like the Mafia, was unable to adapt to changed circumstances. A large, underpopulated continent with apparently limitless natural resources lent itself to exploitation by a combination of competition and increasingly efficient technology, the heart of the free enterprise system. Production and the material well-being it generates became a single goal, and nothing produces quite like that mix of competition and improving technology. Finding its ethical justification in the simplistic socio-biological model of Herbert Spencer's Social Darwinism, the free enterprise system proved adaptive enough until the 1960's, when the United States ceased in its own view to be underpopulated and it became obvious that our non-renewable resources were not without limits. What had not been anticipated was the extraordinary wastefulness of the competitive model attached to efficient technology, and how its voracious consumption of energy and other resources would soon make the whole American economy hopelessly dependent on the economy of the entire planet. Suddenly we found our lives inextricably bound to low-probability systems grandly out of scale, the first humans to experience a kind of exaggerated, built-in randomness. Where once our technology seemed to give us control and establish order, now its grotesque scale, bottomless appetite for resources, and Rube Goldberg complexity actually generates chaos. Think of those Americans who decided to tour Russia to avoid terrorism, and arrived in Kiev just in time for the explosion of the Chernobyl nuclear plant.

It is very difficult to live in this unique time of manufactured randomness, where what we do does not make us proud for long, and what we choose so often turns into something else so quickly we hardly notice it. One thinks of farmers. Farmers, urged on by official government policy moved to larger and larger acreages with more and more expensive technology, borrowing heavily by mortgages on their land and buildings and machinery from banks delighted to oblige, and the Arabs raised the price of oil, and the Russians quit buying grain and the grain yield of other countries grew at lower prices, and the value of American farm land decreased and the banks got nervous and called in their mortgages and farmers who were briefly richer than they had ever been in their lives suddenly lost their farms or had to sell them to agribusiness corporations which were part of larger multinational corporations owned perhaps by Germans or Japanese. My example may be simplistic or inaccurate, but it is no more bizarre and complex than what actually happened during the past two decades. Large, low-probability systems held perilously together by computers and statistics and mindless greed are rapidly doing away with the American farmer, who twenty years ago was boasting that he was the most sophisticated and productive farmer in the world. The Amish, however, are doing very well.

The same kind of sad history can be written of our nuclear energy industry, our automobile industry, our air lines, and our steel industry. Even our computer industry has so many ups and downs that no one in it knows whether they will be working for the same company, or at all, a year from now.

So much for a deregulated world of low-probability systems held together by high technology. Human beings trying to build any kind of normal community within the randomness and unpredictability of such systems tend to get discouraged and exhausted and depressed, or to become adaptive baracudas like Ivan Boesky.

The technology that once served us, that guarded us from a nature perceived as predatory and demanding, that seemed to shorten the mile and expand the hour until immortality seemed almost within our grasp, has bound us suddenly to random change. It has made us the creature and captive of low-probability systems, one of which, our nuclear deterrent, has been created for the sole purpose of threatening to destroy the world in order to avoid the destruction of the world. Technology which, like the Mafia, had once been adaptive, has suddenly become addictive. We find ourselves unable to do without something which is killing us. Technology continuously makes us offers we can't refuse. Genetic engineering. Star Wars. The "crack" of technological addiction.

Shortly before my colonoscopy took place, the nuclear power plant in Chernobyl exploded. The event was an object lesson in the role of denial in low-probability systems. Nuclear plants, like nuclear defense systems and space programs, are triumphs of negative feedback. Every function of the system is monitored and protected from intrusive phenomena which might cause malfunction, by sensors which report to back-up systems to take over if the malfunction is not avoided. Everything is fail-safe. The human beings who monitor these systems are even more complex

55

and unpredictable than the systems themselves, but their negative feedback is primarily designed to protect *them*, although it can also serve the safety of the system where it is identified with human safety.

The identification of those who manage and serve these systems with the systems themselves can be to a degree assumed until the unpredictable happens. At this point the humans lose this identification in a moment and lose all perspective on this system about to become their enemy. There is the rush of fear, followed by the negative feed-back of denial. To avoid utter, runaway panic, the manager denies that what is happening is happening — both to himself, and to the authorities he should report to. This is precisely what happened at Three Mile Island. The mayor of Harrisburg, the governor of Pennsylvania, blandly announced that there was nothing to fear on the basis of what information they could extract from the authorities there. On Public Radio I recently heard a replay of the tape of an NRC expert who finally got into the plant. "Holy Shit!" he shouted, and burst into tears.

Shortly after the worst news (not particularly accurate news) hit the media, ten thousand people jumped into their cars and left the area. Since Three Mile Island is not too densely populated, such a mass evacuation was possible, at least for those with cars and money for shelter. In Chernobyl, located in a totalitarian country with superb public transportation and an elaborate system of government summer camps for families with children, the Russians were able to evacuate 100,000 people in a short time and provide them with adequate quarters until plans could be made for their resettlement and re-employment.

The radiation at Three Mile Island was largely contained and the radiation danger to the surrounding population was apparently negligible. The danger was in the very real possibility that the malfunction would go beyond what could be contained. In that case there would have been a disaster on the level of Chernobyl, but with no centralized public transportation system, no government family camps, no socialized medicine. When one translates this disaster to Plymouth or to Amesbury, Massachusetts in mid-summer, or to Long Island, the chaotic outcome challenges the imagination.

One can't help but imagine irradiated citizens lined up at hospital admissions offices arguing about their health insurance, trying to talk a motel into letting them stay even though they had left credit cards and cash behind, or crowded into their parents' condominium with three kids several months after the explosion, with no job and their health insurance expiring. But most of all, one can't help but imagine thousands of people trapped in gridlock, the radiation descending upon their cars.

This is, of course, precisely what will happen when the first nuclear plant goes. And when it goes, or after it goes, the cause will be, no doubt, determined to be human error. A part of the plant will have missed inspection, or some duct will have been identified as faulty or worn, but the report will have been lost or ignored.

The monitoring of large systems is the most boring job in the world. One is endlessly involved with the electronic report of detail. Every day is the same, and one hopes that every day *will* be the same. Those willing to take on such crushing boredom are not first class engineers, or even mechanics. They often have no theoretical understanding of the system they serve. They learn a procedure and they do it. Even the engineers involved are no shining lights in their profession; there is for engineers more money, and certainly more excitement, to be found elsewhere.

It is a hard job to spend one's days watching endlessly for something to go wrong, or rather, for the *report* of something having gone wrong. This slight distance between the observer and the malfunction, even if a claxon is set off, always leaves room for the denial. How long did it take for the voice of the man monitoring the panel reporting the last flight of Challenger, chanting the numbers, to register at first annoyance and disbelief, and finally, fear, at what the numbers reported? The person monitoring, sitting in the immaculate control room of a high tech enterprise, experiences no change in the environment, when a gauge begins to hint at trouble on the way. Everything is the same. Everything is always the same. How could anything be wrong?

II. THE LANGUAGE OF DEATH: STAYING ALIVE

How could anything go wrong? This question often
follows what has become one of the most often-used phrases
in the American vocabulary: "I can't *believe* this!" We Americans tend to indulge ourselves in fantasies of high tech,
which are usually fantasies of control. We (or at least, I)
imagine brilliant doctors, scientists, and engineers talking a
precise, specialized language as they move with utter assurance within their technology, accomplishing wonderful
things as they hold the disorder of the world at bay. My
colonoscopy destroyed this fantasy forever. It is a procedure
done without anaesthesia, and one is conscious, intensely
conscious, of the conversation going on among the team.
"I'll be darned if I can see it." "Maybe you went by it."
"O.K., let's go back a ways. Shove on his abdomen, will
you? Oh, wow, look at the size of that sucker. Looks like it's
got three heads." "Did you get it?" "Not all of it. I think I got
some of it. Let's go back again and take another look. Ah.
There's the part I missed. I'll get you this time, you little
sucker, you!" And so it went as the doctor traveled event-
fully down my colon like a latterday Huck Finn.

It sounded more to me like a bunch of kids fishing and
fooling around than like the latest high tech procedure for
the early identification of colonic cancer. By the same token,

employees at the Pilgrim nuclear plant were observed throwing a ball of oily rags around the control room. Physicists at the Harvard cyclotron have been fined for eating their lunch in a high radiation area. When people are involved in procedures related to disaster, they develop ways to distance themselves from those procedures. A kind of pseudo-psychic immune system is developed out of regression and denial. It may protect them from severe psychic pain or even madness, but it does not protect them from the actual event they fear.

At the heart of this regression and denial is a great hunger for omnipotent parents — the God-father, the scientist-doctor, the charismatic politician, or, for that matter, the charismatic minister or rabbi. When my doctor started talking like a Cub Scout in the middle of my colonoscopy, my heart sank.

Providentially, one of the projects I was involved in during my interim period was developing a course entitled "Counseling Theory and the Practice of Parish Ministry." There is currently going on in the field of pastoral theology a reevaluation of the dependency of parish ministers on psycho-therapeutic theory. My course was not concerned with counseling, but with the extent to which psychothera-peutic assumptions about human nature govern the deci-sions and actions of ministers as they go about the various functions of parish ministry: committee work, fund raising, preaching, etc.

As I worked on my weekly lectures it became increasingly clear to me that many of these assumptions were inappropri-ate, creating self-fulfilling expectations that worked against the intentions of the minister, while subtly contradicting certain theological givens of Christianity.

However one basic concept of Sigmund Freud, largely ignored in the Church, I found to be both incontrovertible and theologically sound, the concept of transference-countertransference. Whether a minister is called Reverend, Pastor, or Father, (women priests in the Episcopal Church are not yet called Mother, although this title is occasionally considered and often used not quite in jest) the minister is always *in loco parentis*. Many ordained ministers today are rebelling against this role, using human potential psychology's insistence that the healthy human being is "autonomous" (from the Greek, "a law unto oneself"). I do wonder what healthy human-potential therapists do with their autonomy as they are faced with the form presented them by their surgeon absolving the hospital of all responsibility for bad outcomes of the surgery. One can, of course, refuse to sign and turn down the procedure, but as my doctor said to me when I brought up this alternative, "That would seem to me inadvisable."

What one actually does is to scan the walls for impeccable diplomas as one tells oneself, "This doctor is probably the greatest living G.I. specialist. This doctor will do everything in his power to keep me safe, to protect me from pain and suffering and death. Mommy, Daddy, save me." What one actually does is regress, and out of one's regression fall into a sudden, powerful transference to one's doctor. If one was lucky in one's parents, the transference will be positive and one will transfer the trust one had in one's parents onto the doctor. Otherwise the transference may be negative, while just as powerful, particularly today when many doctors, like many ministers, reject being placed *in loco parentis* and explain in percentage terms what the chances are of unpredictable outcomes. Patients are expected to make choices, to take responsibility for their own treatment, and to realize that they are hiring a technician to do a specific job for them in an area which can be full of surprises, including "human error."

"O.K., Buster," the patient with the negative transference says to himself, "but one little mistake and you're going to see me or my heirs in court!" When I asked my doctor if the hospital form didn't bring a lot of anxiety into the doctor-patient relationship, he replied, "You'd be amazed. Some patients get positively paranoid."

So much for autonomy. The astronaut waiting for lift-off, the patient awaiting surgery, the steel worker in Pennsylvania laid off because of low wages in Korea, the American farmer wondering how the Chernobyl disaster will affect the price of his wheat, an indeterminate number of Russians exposed to an "abnormal" amount of radiation and wondering about their private futures — none of these people has any illusions as to his or her autonomy. Life in a postmodern world of immense low-probability systems reduces autonomy to a dream state. Technology has infantilized us. The issue is not autonomy. The issue is trust.

Currently both ministers and doctors are in serious trouble with their constituencies, I suspect, because they are dealing with people whose normal state, due to an addictive dependency on denial, is regressive. Children trust — those who do — because their parents have created for them early on a predictable environment; it meets their needs while disciplining their impulses. The adult who depends unduly on denial is trying to construct or maintain the predictability of the same happy childhood on a foundation of illusion. Such an environment depends on trustworthy parents, parents who can be counted on to keep one safe. The regressed person, building such an illusory world, is constantly in search of parents and hence vulnerable to powerful irrational flights of transference.

Doctors and ministers have always depended on normal transference as a healthy part of the dynamic of their callings. In a stable world, it is no more than the assumption of the trustworthiness of their motives: "If you can't trust a minister, who can you trust?" The public persona of the doctor — grave, kindly, concerned, but distant — enhanced the cohesive mythology of every community. But when denial and regression became endemic in the population, a defense against the growing anxiety generated by the systemic randomness of our corporate life, ministers and doctors suddenly found themselves faced with a new and destructive form of transference. They became the focus of impossible expectations and demands, and where those expectations and demands were not met, of violent hostility. As ministers used to say in the Sixties, "The first year you can do no wrong. The second year you can do no right. The third year, they don't care *what* you do." In the Seventies, ministers began to find themselves being forced out of their parishes by the third or fourth year. Doctors found themselves being sued for malpractice. Both professions have been attempting, unsuccessfully, to restructure their relationships to their constituencies.

Since Ronald Reagan's coming to office, some politicians and some corporation managers, and, in all truth, some evangelical ministers, have discovered a gold mine in this new social phenomenon. They have dropped the low profile and willingly taken on the mantle of parenthood. They become mentors, coaches, confident patriarchs. They simply enter into the fantasy of the regressed and denying person, promise a safe and predictable world and, through personal appearances on television, create the illusion that they are actually building the world they promise. This is not, on the part of these politicians, the sinister manipulation of a battered, frightened, and confused people. Most of these politicians, men in the classically patriarchal role, particularly President Reagan himself, are as attached to this runaway unreality as their constituencies. The dynamic here is counter-transference, the parent figure letting himself be defined by the expectations of his worshippers, sharing their dream of his omnipotence. This transferential charisma is as old as Greek tragedy. The *hubris*, the fatal pride of the leader, led to *athe*, madness, a madness visited upon the leader by a jealous god and finally to nemesis. Agamemmnon, however, was not tied into global systems. The nemesis was local, and the balanced integrity of the polis was restored in the serene Apollonian vision which followed the Dionysian madness and catastrophe of the leader. (Think of the Marshall Plan that followed on the downfall of Hitler.)

If what T.S. Eliot said was true and human beings cannot bear very much reality, the saying becomes even more

64

striking in a time when the reality we are asked to bear contains within it the possibility of ultimate nemesis. In the past, the madness of leaders and their people inexorably played itself out with untold suffering, but always with the expectation of corporate rebirth once the cost of the madness had been paid. The wise, the chorus of elders too old to effect any change in the direction of things, could see precisely where it would all end. They could speak the truth because a part of their wisdom was the knowledge that life with all its possibilities would begin again, once the cost in suffering had been paid.

The elders of our time have no such assurance. I heard a scientist in his late eighties, a Nobel Laureate, address a church group on nuclear war. "I am almost ninety," he said, "and I shall die soon. But many of you, sitting here, will experience nuclear war." For him, old and close to death, the future held no promise whatsoever. He had the calm, Apollonian vision of the wise elder. He had been at the heart of power, been in on the creation of the atom bomb, advised presidents. He spoke calmly and precisely about the specific insanities of the nuclear policy of the Reagan Administration. Like the chorus of elders from time immemorial he watched, clear-eyed but without hope the inexorable progress of *athe* towards nemesis.

On bad days I found myself at sixty-two thinking the same way. I have lived a long life without undue suffering. If it is cancer at an advanced stage, at least I shall not be present at the final agony of the world. Perhaps it is a gift that I shall be spared that, that I shall have only my own death to die. But then I would say to myself, "You fool, you don't know that you have cancer, and you don't know that the world will be destroyed, but what you are learning is that you have no power over either of these possibilities and they are quite separate things. You may have cancer and the world may repent and be saved. Or you may not have cancer and live to see this repentance, or for that matter, nuclear war. The one thing you and the world have in common is the sense of powerless waiting and ambivalent expectation. With this you must live until your life's end."

The Oxford English Dictionary under definition C. defines patience this way: "The calm abiding of the issue of time ... the quality of expecting long without rage or discontent." I suppose no other virtue is in such disrepute in our time. We tend to confuse patience with passivity; while autonomy is reckoned to be the highest level of psychic health, passivity is regarded as a shameful form of pathology. Self-starting, assertive, decisive movers and shakers are regarded as models of mental health, despite the fact that in low-probability systems such people will have very little to say about the outcome of what they start, the consequences of what they assert and decide, or the results of their moving and shaking. At best they will be lucky, at worst, unlucky. In only a few cases will they be held responsible for what is clearly bad luck (no one could have predicted it), but they will be respected and regarded as winners for their good luck. Ronald Reagan was not held responsible for the dip in European tourism or the cost of security for the celebration of the Statue of Liberty in New York. He is praised for proving that America stands tall again by forcing our allies to at least an oral agreement to joint sanctions against terrorism.

This kind of self-centered, risk-taking, "can-do," "no problem" behavior motivated consciously by the will to win and at a deeper level by the fear of death, by an image of the self as survivor, is not without its rationalization. The Polish writer Czeslaw Milosz maintains that the modern world has substituted biology for culture. "You promised us social-ism," he said to the Polish Minister of Culture just before he defected to the West. "You gave us a vulgar Darwinism." The major social purpose of a culture which derives from a religious center is to mitigate the fear of death, to maintain the rational dimension of this fear. However we substitute for culture a reductionist version of natural selection as the essential dynamic of a progressive and productive society, we make the fear of death the central motivational factor. "If I don't get in the 600's on my S.A.T.'s, I'm dead." "If Mondale doesn't get the women's vote, he's dead." Or in the latest and most vivid mortal metaphor, "You cross Ronald Reagan once, and you're dead meat." Where biology is substituted for culture, not to win is to lose, not to succeed is to fail, not to keep growing is to start dying. "Winning," as President Nixon used to say, quoting Vince Lombardi, "is not the most important thing. Winning is the *only* thing."

In such a cultureless, biological environment, there is little room for patience. "The calm abiding of the issue of time" would, by this view, make one a sitting duck. All we can expect of time is death, but if we are winners then we can make a Faustian bargain and receive a comfortable stay of execution. Fitness to survive is all, and since survival in its biological sense is itself an illusory goal (we *don't* survive, we no longer have a guarantee that even our genes will survive) it follows that winning, surviving, and succeeding are not helpful or realistic metaphors for the long term.

Patience is, of course, a long-term virtue, a virtue rooted in a culture which assumes generational continuity and a good end for the human endeavor. In our own time of "rage and discontent" we are obsessed with change, or liberation, or growth — inner or outer, spiritual or existential. For the present that we live in seems to provide so much less than what we need to be secure, to be a winner, a survivor. Hypermotivated by fear, feeling no long-term identification with history, which may itself end abruptly at any time, isolated from all corporate belonging by the failure of any consensus about the nature of the common good, the biological human being, even though he or she may seem like a particularly competent and successful professional, will answer, when asked how things are going, "Surviving." All that energy to "stay alive."

It may very well be that we are the first society to make raw fear the primary motivation of our life together, and to see fear as a good and healthy motivation, indeed, at the heart of a dynamic and progressive society. Granted our reliance on denial as our chief defense, we do not think of our fear as the fear of death — except metaphorically. We are more inclined to depend on the fear of failure, the fear of losing, the fear of deprivation and diminishment, the fear of rejection and excommunication, the fear of ridicule, the fear of weakness, sickness, abnormality, abandonment, ugliness, obesity, aging. Advertisers, politicians, the news media, even teachers work on these fears constantly to keep us motivated to buy, to invest, to compete, to work, to play, to "get ahead" or, at least, "to stay alive." Survival is the magic word. "We're not talking frills here, we're not talking options, we're not talking what would be nice. We're talking *survival*. We're talking bottom line. We do this, baby, or we're dead meat."

We hear this anxious line of argument at corporation board meetings, or at Little League parents' meetings, in reference to SALT II or hiring a new coach for the high school basketball team. Ministers talk this way to their boards of deacons, parents to their children. The language can be less crude, or a great deal more crude, but the message is clear and the same in every case. The most important and significant reason for doing one thing rather than another, indeed, the only reason for doing anything involving the most minimal risk or commitment is to survive. At times this concern for survival can be extended to a group one is involved with beyond one's immediate family, but for the most part, increasingly, survival is an individual matter.

A daughter calls her father from college to tell him she has decided to major in the classics. His response may be something like this: "I know that you loved Latin in High School, and I'm sure that the classics are a good thing and you should certainly take some courses in them, but let's face it, kid, this is 1987 and it's a whole new ball game. You might marry some nice guy who'll take care of you for the rest of your life, but that is getting more and more unlikely. I mean let's be realistic about this, dear. It's a jungle out there.

Nobody gives a damn whether you live or die. When you leave college I can't go on supporting you forever. You're going to have to get out there and cut it with the rest of them. Classics won't do it. You better start thinking right now about what you're going to do to survive. I mean I'm putting an arm and a leg into your education because I know how important it is if you're going to make it. Don't do something now you're going to feel sorry for when it's too late. I mean, if you want to major in classics, that's *your* business, but remember, paying the bills is *my* business. Think about it!"

As a college chaplain I heard this lecture, or one very like it, related to me by a fair number of students. The father says, "Let's be realistic." If he's talking to a son, the argument is more radical. "Come on, kid. When are you going to *face reality*," he shouts angrily. What is meant by reality here is biological reality, a poor, reductionist biological theory of natural selection and the survival of the fittest. Again, if it is a father talking to his son, he may very well add, "You major in the classics and you're dead. I'm not spending all this money to create one more loser."

The language of death comes easily to the tongue of the American male, and increasingly to the tongue of the American professional woman. It expresses naturally and powerfully the biological paradigm by which we are taught from childhood to make sense out of life. This paradigm is communicated to us with great urgency and power as we go through the screening process of American education, the standardized testing and laning, leading inexorably to the apocalypse of the S.A.T.'s, all this accompanied by the chorus of elders chanting, "You blow this one, babe, and you're dead."

Competition for survival is not, perhaps, the best motivation to bring to the randomness and unpredictability of life in low-probability systems. Deregulation — freeing a lot of scared people up to cut each others' throats — is perhaps not the most helpful approach to a corporate life which has become at best chaotic as the rich get richer and crazier and the poor get poorer and angrier, as human error asserts itself in ever more destructive ways and human terror becomes a vocation of the disinherited, and both have a new importance and significance in the grand low-probability systems that high technology provides for us to live in.

III. THE BODY IN PAIN

Patience. "The calm abiding of the issue of time ... the quality of expecting long without rage or discontent." Four months seems like a long time to find out whether one has cancer or not. In a curious way, you are not motivated to speed it up by an aggressive assault on your health care system because it seems easier to live with the possibility that the polyp is benign, than to deal with the hard fact that it is malignant. Nothing has changed, you tell yourself. Even five years ago you simply would not have known you *had* a polyp; at that time one's faeces were not examined for blood in a routine physical. (Blessings on you, President Reagan). Yet the consciousness of the possibility of malignancy cannot be erased. Wouldn't it be easier to deal with cancer, something concrete, than with the possibility of cancer? After all, if one's polyp is deemed malignant by the pathology lab, then it has been malignant inside of one all those many months. Yet one doesn't (or at least I didn't) press for a verdict, demand a clear yes or no. Indeed, I began to like what an intensification of the indeterminancy of being alive did to my daily life. It did not make me happy. At times it made me moderately unhappy. Samuel Johnson's concentration of the mind seems to come closest to describing what I liked about my interior state. My mind was not concentrated *on* death, as I assume Dr. Johnson must have intended. It was led *by* death to concentrate on a number of things more usually ignored or put aside, or to perceive the necessary and ordinary concerns of the day differently.

The most obvious center of concentration is the body. The existence of a colonic polyp does not itself affect the body in any way that one is conscious of. Everything goes on the same as before. The sigmoidoscopy, the lower G.I. X-Ray, bring abstract results, words, pictures, and symbols of the thing. It is like the high tech engineer monitoring the gauges of Three Mile Island. There is something ominous there, but nothing has changed for *me*. One is not driven to the doctor by painful symptoms, but by having given one's consent to a pro-forma physical, an annual technological extension of one's immune system. Like the ancients, we find ourselves examining the entrails to predict the future. Perhaps the movement towards technology is a movement towards the barbarous.

Certainly any conviction I had about the falseness of distinguishing between mind and body is put to the test. The body becomes flesh, a carcass, a thing one drags around as necessary, an object. The mind seems free to become obsessed with this object, or to concern itself with something else, or to relate this object to something else. The last is experienced as controlling the body by mind and will, something which, by the canons of holism, we are not supposed to imagine ourselves doing. Perhaps we experience it this way because our language won't permit us to experience it otherwise.

I found Elaine Scarry's book, *The Body in Pain*, helpful here. She substitutes the contemporary concepts of voice and body for the traditional theological ones of word and flesh. Mind, for me, has always been voice. I read aloud to myself. My wife says she can see my throat working as I read. I address myself constantly with great floods of words. During the time of my mortal concentration, I found myself lecturing and preaching to my body, about my body, and of course from my body. The voice reveals itself by a particular larynx. It is a product of the body upon which it comments so endlessly. Werner Erhardt of EST fame is often quoted by his followers to the effect that "suffering is the story you tell yourself about your pain."

According to Elaine Scarry, God in the Old Testament is a voice seeking a body, which he finds in the New Testament. The word becomes flesh. The voice becomes body. Yet the intensification of one's knowledge that one is mortal tends to separate one's voice from one's body. The voice turns upon the body and accuses it of mortality. The body dumbly ignores the voice and slouches towards death at its own pace, captive to its genes, doing as it is told, not by the voice, but by the laws of biology. The voice again becomes disincarnate, a harmless and useless kvetch, which echoes, dissipates and disappears into the dark tunnel of time past.

As I thought about, as I voiced to myself this anxious disincarnation of my voice, it seemed to me that I became aware of how oblivious my body was to the voice which, after all, issued from that same body which ignored it. It seemed to me that the developed nations and perhaps the planet itself had become separate from their voice. Any coherent culture has a voice through which it addresses and by which it shapes each new generation. Fourth and fifth century Athens was addressed and shaped by its great playwrights, philosophers, sculptors, architects, and politicians. The cumulative wisdom of this cultural voice, this *paideia*, defined what it was to be human in Athens during these centuries.

In the United States after the revolution the cultural voice which addressed and shaped our society through the founders and the constitution was the voice of John Locke. To be born and raised an American up until the late nineteenth century was to be addressed and formed constantly by the voice of John Locke and other philosophers of the enlightenment.

Today none of the developed nations respond to any coherent cultural voice. Instead, they react as swiftly and adaptively as they can to the random trauma of runaway technological change. Nothing speaks to them, nothing addresses them, to affect what they do.

Langdon Winner begins his book *Autonomous Technology* with two quotes. The first is from Werner Heisenberg's *Physics and Philosophy*:

> The enormous success of this combination of natural and technical science led to a strong preponderance of those nations or states or communities in which this kind of activity flourished, and, as a natural consequence of this activity had to be taken up even by those nations which by tradition would not have been inclined toward natural and technological sciences. The

modern means of communication and of traffic finally completed this process of expansion of technical civilization. Undoubtedly the process has fundamentally changed the conditions of life on earth; and whether one approves of it or not, whether one calls it progress or danger, one must realize that it has gone far beyond any control through human forces. One may rather consider it a biological process on the largest scale whereby the structures active in the human organism encroach on larger parts of matter and transform it into a state suited for the increasing human population.

The second quote is from Martin Heidegger's *Discourse on Thinking*:

No one can foresee the radical changes to come. But technological advance will move faster and faster and can never be stopped. In all areas of his existence, man will be encircled ever more tightly by the forces of technology. These forces, which everywhere and every minute claim, enchain, drag along, press and impose upon man under the form of some technical contrivance or other — these forces ... have moved long since beyond his will and have outgrown his capacity for decision.

The words which leap out of Heisenberg's passage are, "Whether one approves of it or not, whether one calls it progress or danger, one must realize that it has gone far beyond any control through human forces."

77

Again, the disincarnate voice. The voice is yelping at the heels of the great deaf body of corporate life as it moves randomly ahead, devouring the last of its sustenance, like an addict whose largest dose is always the one which finishes off his supply. "Progress!" the voice calls. "Danger!" the voice calls. Progress without any conscious teleology. Danger with such a huge list of threats as to be meaningless. The beast mindlessly lunges ahead obedient only to its D.N.A., addressed by no other voice.

Heidegger's bleak view of a technologically dominated future, has the same tone of biological inexorability: these forces ... have *outgrown* [our] capacity for decision." Growth, like winning or succeeding, has taken on a strange metaphorical power in our time. Not to grow is to die, or, worse yet, to be dead. Concepts of maturity and of diminishment are ignored. Personal growth, spiritual growth, economic growth, are all good things. The price one pays for growth is change. Anyone who is unable or unwilling to change will not grow, and consequently will die, or is already "dead." Anyone who is not growing cannot be a winner. There is a massive distrust in our time of any steady state, any homeostasis. Anything is possible to one open to change and growth, which are the two conditions of maximum adaptivity and assured survival.

Yet when I discovered that I had a "growth," I was not pleased. There is the frightening side of growth. We hear that communism is a "cancerous growth" on human corporate existence, or that the Mafia is a "tumor" on the body social. Even population growth can be presented as a planetary cancer. How one sees growth seems to be a matter of mood, but one thing becomes increasingly certain. Whatever one begins, plants, or initiates in low-probability systems, grows — if it grows — according to its own laws, or some law of randomness. Its outcome will not be what was intended in its initiation, and whatever its shape, size, or rate of growth, whatever the purpose for which it was originally intended, it will end up if it continues struggling blindly to stay alive, unaddressed by any universal voice, oblivious to its vital dependence on the corporate life around it.

All growth in the corporate life of humans, unaddressed by voice, seems to become cancerous in time.

As I would listen to President Reagan address the various catastrophic events which kept forcing themselves upon my consciousness during those four months, I was astonished at the distance between his voice and the events themselves. Mr. Reagan understands the proper responsibility of a president to articulate and interpret events which may affect or even shape the national consciousness. No president since Roosevelt has taken this responsibility more seriously or has done it technically so well.

The president's highest praise goes to those marines, flyers, or astronauts who "did what they had to do." When he explains why he instigates something which seemed to many, perhaps most people, irrational, like the bombing of Tripoli, he says with great conviction, "We did what had to be done."

I think this phrase originally had to do with a code of honor. A gentleman had no choice when his face was slapped with a glove, but to arrange for a duel. Yet the president makes no reference to honor. The results are strangely self-contradictory. Freedom, the president's first value, is freedom to do what you have to do, to give in to the iron rule of natural selection whatever its consequences. Not to do what you have to do is to be shamefully destroyed. To do what you have to do is to win or lose, to take one's place as a "player" in the great scheme of progress towards what Herbert Spencer called "the perfect man in the perfect society," the evolving great republic of the future.

The voice of the president exists in a vacuum, unrelated to events. It takes no responsibility for these events as they, and the human beings who bring them to fruition or catastrophe, do what is required of them. They do what they "have" to do in a cosmic war which the president sometimes sees, as Hobbes did, as a war of all against all, and sometimes with Marx as a war of "us against them." In all fairness, Hobbes at least saw the war of all against all, and life itself as "solitary, poor, nasty, brutish, and short," as the conditions of a pure state of nature from which humans could be rescued by three forces: fear, hope, and reason. Mr. Reagan, beneath his rhetoric, believes fear will do it. At a press conference a reporter asks, "Mr. President, our European allies are complaining that there is no basis in reality for so many Americans staying away from Europe this summer out of their fear of terrorism. Would you comment, please?" The president replies that he would not want to be quoted as urging Americans to go into a situation that was potentially dangerous. Another reporter states that many Americans fearing terrorism, were going to stay away from the celebration at the Statue of Liberty. "Well," the president replies, "it would be a tempting target!"

As I sat listening to this voice from my T.V. it occurred to me that President Reagan's message was, simply stated, over and over again, "Life is fearfully dangerous, but don't worry. I'm your president and will keep you safe." This phrase finds its sacramental expression in Star Wars. "You can trust me as a good father to shelter you from danger. As for the dangers beneath Star Wars' dome, play the game. Winners win big. But if you lose, you're dead. All human worth is in doing what has to be done."

It is not immediately apparent to many people why a teacher *had* to be sent into space, why Tripoli *had* to be bombed, or why so much of the national budget *must* go to pay for the president's fantasies of cosmic security as expressed in Star Wars. Yet as the president and as increasing numbers of people see it, there was no choice. As they say at M.I.T., "What *can* be done, *will* be done." Voices cackle like static around the human enterprise, which lumbers deafly on.

It occurred to me, as I contemplated the possibility of malignant growth in my own colon, that human beings have the least trustworthy D.N.A. of all. Birds know how to be birds, ants know how to be ants, trees know how to be trees, but human beings haven't a clue about being human if they're not told. To be human they must hear a voice, and the voice must be trustworthy. The voice speaks not through D.N.A. but through culture. Humankind cannot be humankind apart from a culture which speaks with a coherent and trustworthy voice that defines over and over again for each

81

generation what it is to be human. From this, humanity learns what one does to be human, and, finally, why it is important or significant to *be* human and do human things.

It is a truism, yet nevertheless true, that Copernicus and Galileo removed us from the center of the universe, that Newton removed any hope of our immortality, that Darwin placed us firmly among the animals, and Freud removed any illusions we had about our free will. All this was the price we paid to manage our planetary environment by science and technology. But the latest source of damage to our corporate self-esteem has no author, no identifiable voice. High technology issues from no person. As Heisenberg says, "It has gone far beyond any control through human forces." What was begun as intentional, as a kind of sacramental proof of human mastery, has taken on a life of its own, existing for its own sake in order to be served by its creators.

Or so it seems. But one can't help but ask oneself why it seems this way. What is the compulsion here? Why do we, as the president likes to put it, "have to do what we have to do"? The answer that emerged from my four months of mortal concentration was simple enough. It is because in this bizarre century we are inordinately afraid of death, not merely of our own death, but the death of our species and perhaps of all organic life. We have become a body divorced from voice, a walking heap of entropy, as we have come to understand and define ourselves. A human body, social or individual, separated from voice, not spoken to or spoken for, and itself dumb, obedient only to the single fear of its particular death, a fear built into its genes and unmitigated by the voice which speaks through a coherent and ordering culture, to, for, and from the body itself. This body goes its way motivated entirely by fear without hope or reason, addicted to whatever once served its survival, blind to its environment, unaware of its eco-dependence, destroying whatever might sustain it, friendless, alien, alone, and, always, dying in its massive, mindless attempt to survive.

In the absence of any cultural voice to mitigate our fear of death, we find ourselves turning to other sources of consolation. Another public theme which became more and more persistent and urgent during those four months that I waited was the matter of drugs. It seems there was an escalating war against drugs by the Reagan Administration, a war which, one was constantly informed, the Administration was losing. There were two prongs to the Reagan offensive. The purpose of the first was to interdict drug (marijuana and cocaine) traffic from South American sources, and the purpose of the second was education— mainly in the form of information about what the drugs did to those who used them. During the Sixties, when I had been a college chaplain, I had informed myself about drugs as a part of my job. Since then the only "new" drug is cocaine—new in its increasing use. I had known cocaine users in Greenwich Village in the Forties but they had been a part of village exotica, or else jazz musicians. Cocaine was the only drug at that time which was generally regarded as dangerous by drug users themselves. It generated, they said, a powerful short-term hypermanic high followed by an abysmal crash. Even heroin users insisted that cocaine was something to be avoided. It puzzled me that it should suddenly have become so fashionable, particularly among middleclass professionals.

Of all the reading I have done about drugs, far and away the most useful has been the essay on addiction with which William Burroughs begins *Naked Lunch*. Heroin, Burroughs writes, is the ideal capitalist product because it creates its own market. Prophetic words indeed. As the information poured in from the media it became more and more obvious that marijuana and cocaine were now a significant economic issue, built into the structure of American economic life as a quick and easy source of capital formation. For developing South American countries, marijuana and even more, cocaine, have become a kind of economic high. This was particularly true because the Russians have shut down the smuggling of heroin from Southeast Asia through Afghanistan. Again, it has been a matter of large, low-probability systems. Planes and boats equipped with elegant electronic equipment, quick international transfers of huge amounts of money by computers to Swiss and other unregulated banks, a world economic system so complicated, unpredictable, and beyond human control that it could be entered into at any point—all these things had worked together to make the drug traffic a structural, systemic, economic issue. Now it cannot be dealt with at all without creating an unpredictable array of political and diplomatic, as well as economic, crises.

This leaves education. On a major T.V. station I saw an hourlong educational program devoted entirely to "crack." As a part of this education, the viewer was treated to a detailed demonstration of how cocaine was made into crack by an assortment of addict-pushers in a makeshift laboratory somewhere near New York City. I found it more informative than I had any need for it to be, since I now knew how to make cocaine into crack, which I could not have done before. I think the point of this demonstration had been to show how easy it was to do, and consequently how hard it would be to stop this process with so many small entrepreneurs gainfully employed. How many more entrepreneurs were launched into so profitable a venture by this demonstration it is hard to say.

So much for drug education. Never has so much disinformation, misinformation, and irrelevant information saturated a society so quickly in history. The politics of sheer panic has been born. All the instrumental questions have been asked, all the instrumental solutions have been tried. But the question of *inwardness* has been studiously, carefully, avoided. What is there that is so painful about the inner life of Americans that needs to be transformed into comfortable illusion? What horrendous thing is going on inside such a person — even a person with a college degree and some sophistication — which would make that person risk using cocaine to deal with it?

There is no reasoning, no cognitive dimension, to anyone over the age of fifteen trying a hard drug. It is an act of pure impulse, triggered by chronic inward anxiety. It is not until the drug has been taken that the enormity of the anxiety is apprehended, when the drug user experiences for the first time the euphoria of being anxiety-free. The degree to which people will go to do away with anxiety if they *don't* turn to drugs can be seen in the harebrained anti-drug legislation that came close to being passed by Congress; it legitimated illegal search and seizure, a mandatory death penalty for drug-related murder, and the use of the United States Army to defend us from our own.

In this war on drugs education is taken to mean information. Presumably if everyone knew where crack comes from, how it is made and what it does to the nervous system, how it creates addiction, how it threatens life, then people would not start using it or, if they already used it, would seek help in giving up its use. This is the same empirical logic one sees in anti-nuclear education, where it is assumed that if people really understood what nuclear weapons are doing and could do to the world, and to them, they would mobilize for a nuclear freeze or nuclear disarmament. The assumption is that the fear of pain, horror and meaningless death motivates people to behave rationally. The voice rants at the body, but the body is deaf to the voice. Language sputters and cackles and the body "does what it has to do."

As Burroughs saw, it is a matter of systemic addiction. When she has a $10,000.00 stash of heroin in her bureau drawer, the heroin addict gets up and goes cheerfully to work, has a normal social life and partakes of her heroin in a rational and temperate way until the stash is noticeably depleted. At this point she begins to experience anxiety, which she handles by heavier doses of heroin taken ever more frequently. The stash begins to diminish more rapidly. The addict increases the size and frequency of dosage to meet the increase in her anxiety. The addict's voice tells her, "You are killing yourself." Her body tells itself, "My survival depends on the next dose." The body listens to itself, not to the voice.

We see the addictive pattern Burroughs describes here in the shopping patterns of many credit card holders, in the investments of major banks in the Third World, and in the Third World economic wisdom which tells them that the more they owe, the more they can borrow. "We can't go cold turkey." "Just lend us enough to get through this bad patch and when our withdrawal symptoms are worked through we'll quit! And pay you back." We see it perhaps most clearly in the nuclear arms race. In fact it is possible to wonder whether the president's own malignant polyp did not set off a somewhat intensified sense of mortality, an apprehension of his stash of time running out, and a projection of this apprehension on the world. His response to SALT II was curious.

It is now clear that Reagan was not concerned about Soviet violations of SALT II in its unsigned form. Rather he has decided that it is dangerous for the United States to limit any of its options by any form of treaty with the Soviet Union, a decision that is in line with his general theory of deregulation. One does not make agreements with one's adversaries. One pursues one's own interests (survival interests) as an adversary, "doing what has to be done" until nature's providence, by the process of natural selection, sorts out winners and losers. As the stash runs out, the president goes for it with Star Wars, a fantasy generated by survival terror, an elaborate high-tech megasystem designed to make America ultimately safe from nuclear attack. Already Star Wars, like the drug trade or the Mafia, is deeply a part of the world's economic system. Not only the United States, but the whole world, including the Soviet Union, is hooked on

Star Wars. Such enormous sums of money pumped into the world's economy create a mindless universal dependency. This pseudo-immune system will be, if our commitment actually to building it becomes real, like a final, lethal dose of heroin taken to meet the body's last cry for survival. It will push our economy beyond its limits and possibly the Soviets beyond the limits of their forbearance.

In the end, drugs, and not just narcotic drugs, but the whole armamentarium from whiskey to insulin or penicillin, are part and parcel of this same pseudo-immune system. It is an immune system which, while creating the illusion of protecting us from death, does no more than protect us from the fear of death, does no more than make our denial more plausible to us. The more the fear of death is used to motivate us, the more reductionist biology takes the place of culture, the more obsessed we become with our own survival, the more the rational and hopeful dimensions of fear are repressed and the distance between voice and body grows. Our pseudo-immune system takes on a life of its own and betrays the body it was created to defend.

As it turned out, the polyps were benign. The procedure itself was excruciating and traumatic. The demoral-cum-valium didn't come close to helping with the pain. The high-technology went on amidst my screams and the idle chatter of the team. At the end of the procedure, the doctor, pleased as punch, insisted on my looking at the polyps in a small bottle, as though they were my new-born baby.

Then followed two and a half days of waiting, and I remember little of them beyond my irritability. By Monday morning I had become quite aggressive, really pushy on the telephone, as I kept after the doctor's office for results. Finally, around noon, the doctor called to announce cheerfully that there was no sign of malignancy. I thanked him and asked him how soon I could row again after the procedure.

"Row? On the river? Oh. Tomorrow it will be perfectly safe." The next morning I went on my bicycle to the boat club. There had been no rush of joy, no ecstatic sense of liberation at the good news. I began to relate somewhat more consciously to my surroundings, to be aware of the people I met, to return my attention to my ordinary existence in a way I had not for those two days. But there was no rush of gratitude, or relief. This worried me, and I hoped that rowing might put me in touch with some "lightness of being." I had been patient in my expectations, but I had been expectant during those four months. I had expected to be overjoyed by a benign report, a "new lease on life"— what a coldly accurate phrase!

I have rowed a single shell on the Charles River in Cambridge off and on for forty-five years, and out of the boat club since 1963, when I took up rowing again as part of a strategy to give up smoking.

Rowing has a significant place in my life. In its blessed solitude I have composed sermons, come to decisions, worked off stress, dealt with loss, or simply enjoyed the languor of a spring day, the elegant simplicity of the shell so perfectly crafted to be an extension of the human body.

I entered the shell room, logged in, took my sculls down the ramp and laid them on the dock. I returned to the racks of shells, grateful that my favorite, an old Garofalo, was not in use. I heaved the shell off the rack and carried it to the horses on the dock onto which I carefully let it down. I unscrewed the guards on the oar-locks, turned the shell over on to its hull, adjusted the stretcher and put the shell in the water. I put the inboard scull in place and screwed the oarlock guard tight, then the outboard scull. I put my rubber pad on the seat, my right foot on the foot pad and shoved off into the Charles with my left. I distanced myself from the dock with three strokes at half slide and laced my feet into the boots on the stretcher. Every discrete phase of the launching was as automatic as breathing. Ah! The orderliness of ritual.

The day was perfect. The slight northwest breeze hardly ruffled the water and made the sky a vivid blue as it carried the pollution of the Boston area out to sea.

I headed upstream, rowing at a good clip. My body felt good, strong, responsive. It was mine. It was doing what was demanded of it. For the time being. Thank God.

Must "Thank God" be all one has to say after one's mind has wrestled with one's own death for four months? Is there nothing behind all this curious metaphorical interrelatedness between the world and my own inwardness? For there is some kind of order here, invented or created, discovered or projected. The world as I saw it in my mortal concentration was not a heap of events. Surely as a priest and a preacher I must have something more to say than "Thank God" after so much expense of time and spirit. Yet I don't. At least not some systematic, orderly, theological interpretation of all these revelations of order in fits and starts.

The Jesuit, John S. Dunne, writes somewhere that mystery is not the unintelligible. Mystery is the inexhaustibly intelligible. Human life as mystery is seldom appreciated when one is in the midst of career momentum and one's thinking and doing is largely instrumental and strategic. It is some *memento mori* which brings one's existence into question and leads one to ask if life experienced as one damned thing after another is all there is. But what one discovers in one's existence when one asks the question of meaning and order is not some grand master plan or all-inclusive explanatory system. Even St. Thomas Aquinas came to see this as he approached death. What one discovers is rather this inexhaustible intelligibility — fragmentary insights that suggest but do not define or limit a larger order.

If our mode of reflection on this mystery, indeed, our general way of knowing, is exclusively empirical we shall discover in the end only one trustworthy principle, the principle of entropy, the rule of decay and death. We shall discover the body as carcass, voice and culture as maladaptive human substitutes for good genetic information. One exhausts and reduces the intelligibility of human life and planetary life very quickly under the empirical microscope, and life, in Eugene O'Neil's words, becomes "a long day's journey into night."

There are other ways of knowing. One of them, as Peter Elbow points out in his extraordinary essay, "The Doubting Game and the Believing Game," is Tertullian's. "I know because I believe." If one thinks biblically, wihout attempting to extrapolate an abstract system from the Bible to explain everything, one discovers in parables, metaphors, and narrative the same surprising fragments of perception and insight into a larger and inexhaustible order that one discovers in reflecting upon one's own condition, one's own history, one's own daily life, with the added seriousness mortal concentration provides. Indeed, the Bible, particularly as it is read (and occasionally preached on) within the liturgy of the church helps one to reflect upon one's existence in precisely (or imprecisely, with a roomy imprecision) this way.

Perhaps the metaphor of rowing with which I chose to end this piece is too solitary. I was thinking of my body as the church, the Incarnation in sacramental form, its voice and body reconciled. For the church is like a rower, rowing boldly backwards towards the bridge upstream and beyond with only an occasional vision of what lies ahead. She is oriented on the river mainly by what she has left significantly behind.

Still, too solitary. And yet — Thank God! The metaphors are as inexhaustible as the intelligibility of God.

Cowley Publications is a work of the Society of St. John the Evangelist, a religious community for ment in the Episcopal Church. The books we publish are a significant part of our ministry, together with the work of preaching, spiritual direction, and hospitality. Our aim is to provide books that will enrich their readers' religious experience and challenge it with fresh approaches to religious concerns.